WELCOME TO
Wentworth
CHARTERED
1766

Welcome to
HINSDALE

Welcome to:
TOWN OF
HUDSON
SHIRE

Welcome To
Milford
EST. 1794

Welcome to
HAMPTON
BEACH
Village District

TWIN MOUNTAIN
TOWN OF CARROLL
Established
1832

WELCOME TO
DEERING
SETTLED 1765

Welcome to
Freedom

Welcome to
CONTOOCOOK
VILLAGE
EST. 1765

Welcome to
GORHAM
NEW HAMPSHIRE
INCORPORATED
1836

Welcome to
Strafford
New Hampshire

WELCOME TO
BRETTON WOODS
TOWN OF CARROLL
Established
1832

WELCOME TO
LEE
INCORPORATED 1766

INC. 1766
Welcome to
TOWN OF
EATON

WELCOME TO
FITZWILLIAM
Incorporated 1773

Welcome To
WINCHESTER N.H.
INCORPORATED
1753

Welcome to
the VILLAGE of
SALMON FALLS
ROLLINSFORD NH

WELCOME TO
SWANZEY
INCORPORATED 1753

Welcome to
New Hampshire

Ken Paulsen

SCHIFFER
PUBLISHING

Other Schiffer Books by the Author:

Vermont: A Focus on Fall, ISBN 978-0-7643-5155-6
Vermont: An Autumn Perspective, ISBN 978-0-7643-5390-1
New Hampshire: An Autumn Sojourn, ISBN 978-0-7643-3870-0
New Hampshire: A Keepsake, ISBN 978-0-7643-5748-0

Edited by Ian Robertson
Cover design by Molly Shield
Type set in Beutiful ES & Minion

ISBN: 978-0-7643-5749-7
Printed in China

Published by Schiffer Publishing, Ltd.
4880 Lower Valley Road
Atglen, PA 19310
Phone: (610) 593-1777; Fax: (610) 593-2002
E-mail: Info@schifferbooks.com
Web: www.schifferbooks.com

For our complete selection of fine books on this and related subjects, please visit our website at www.schifferbooks.com. You may also write for a free catalog.

Schiffer Publishing's titles are available at special discounts for bulk purchases for sales promotions or premiums. Special editions, including personalized covers, corporate imprints, and excerpts, can be created in large quantities for special needs. For more information, contact the publisher.

We are always looking for people to write books on new and related subjects. If you have an idea for a book, please contact us at proposals@schifferbooks.com.

Table of Contents

Introduction

Welcome to New Hampshire. Whether you are new to the state, a lifelong resident, or one of the millions who choose to vacation here each year, scenes representing New Hampshire's rural character, seasonal events, and year-round activities are on display in this four-season tour of the Granite State.

New Hampshire has been a perennial national top ten choice in many categories, such as health care, education, and quality of life. The friendly people and natural beauty of the landscape make it an ideal vacation spot or permanent residence.

While some states do not experience much annual seasonal change as the calendar months pass, New Hampshire definitely gets a taste of each one. Officially, the calendar can pinpoint the exact date and time when we go from one season to the next; in reality, sometimes a season may begin before and linger after those dates. Golf courses could open in February one year and still have snow on the fairways in April the next. Northern ski slopes generally try to open around Thanksgiving weekend and, with any luck, stay open until late April, sometimes even into May.

In representing the four seasons, it became a decision as to what the cutoff was in each of the chapters. Should it only be based on a calendar date, or should the image itself dictate in which chapter it resides? The second option was chosen for this book.

Featured are images of quaint rural settings, idyllic village scenes, and some of the more than fifty covered bridges found around the state. Typical New Hampshire events are highlighted, such as sled dog racing in winter, maple syrup making in spring, swimming and other water-related activities in summer, and hiking on well-loved trails in fall.

New Hampshire offers a variety of gifts for all to enjoy. Take in the splendor displayed during each season; the welcome sign is out.

Welcome Bienvenue
New Hampshire
LIVE FREE OR DIE

WELCOME TO PORTSMOUTH
SETTLED 1623

Welcome To
Epping
EST. 1741

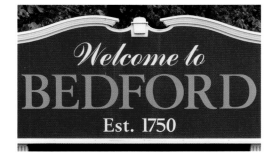

Welcome to
BEDFORD
Est. 1750

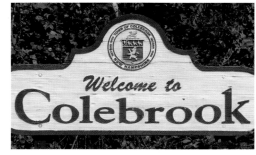

Welcome to
Colebrook

Welcome to
WESTMORELAND
NEW HAMPSHIRE
Incorp. 1752

Welcome to
ROCHESTER
THE LILAC CITY

WELCOME TO DANVILLE

WELCOME TO UNITY

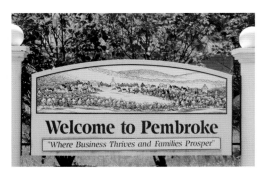

Winter

Winter is perhaps our longest season. Forget the calendar date: winter can begin with a small snow prelude—reacquainting drivers with caution they had forgotten in the prior three seasons—or it may come in a deluge to proclaim, "ready or not, I have arrived!" It can come very early, as it did one year when two feet of snow fell in parts of southern New Hampshire on Halloween, and it can stay late, with the lilac blossoms of mid-May receiving a coating of snow another year.

The bears go into hibernation while skiers come out of their own to frolic on the many mountain slopes scattered around the state. Snowshoeing, cross country skiing, and outdoor hockey rinks offer other outdoor options. Snowmobilers have miles and miles of designated trails, with some of the best spots in the Great North Woods area. Stay at one of the bed and breakfasts and you may have the added pleasure of "dashing through the snow in a one-horse open sleigh."

Spectators gather for events unique to this time of the year. At least three organizations offer sled dog races, typically beginning in late January into March. Ice-harvesting events show how blocks of ice were cut from frozen lakes, covered in sawdust, and stored for summer before the modern refrigerator. Maple sap gathering demonstrates the process of collecting sap and boiling it down to maple syrup. A trip to the ice castle in the Lincoln / North Woodstock area offers a memorable winter experience.

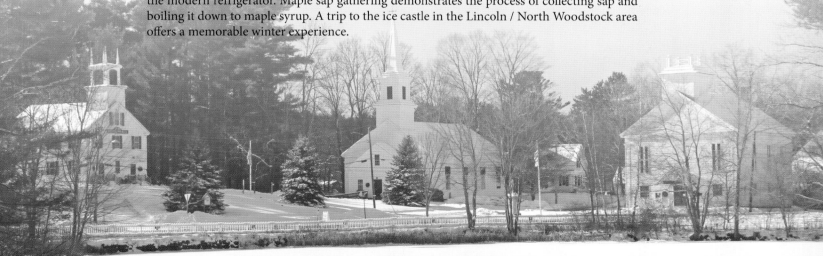

Rindge

Contoocook River, Bennington

Top of Cannon Mountain

Conway Scenic Railroad Depot, North Conway

Milford

Haverhill-Bath Covered Bridge in Woodsville

Omni Mount Washington Resort

Sled dog races in Laconia are a highlight of winter.

A covered bridge in Henniker

Decorated for the holidays

Stone arch bridge in Hillsborough

Atkinson

Flume Covered Bridge with Mount Liberty in the background

The Piscataquog River runs through the center of New Boston.

Marlow

Freestyle skiing began in New Hampshire.

Mount Washington Valley in Conway

Honeymoon Bridge, Jackson

Dashing through the snow in an early snowmobile

Old fashioned sleigh ride at the Farm by the River in North Conway

Inside the ice castle at night

Sullivan

Red barn near Croydon

Sap gathering contest at Stonewall Farm in Keene shows how it used to be done.

Concord

Round barn along Route 10 in Piermont

Ice cut from Kezar Lake in North Sutton gets stored for summer at the Muster Field Farm nearby.

Carleton Covered Bridge, Swanzey

Boiling sap down to maple syrup is a labor of love.

Meredith

Freshly groomed trails await the morning skier on Cannon Mountain.

Sanbornton

Ashuelot Covered Bridge

Hampstead

Exterior view of the ice castle in the North Woodstock / Lincoln area

An ice sculptor prepares the final piece for his contest entry.

Dorchester old school house

Spring

As the sun takes a longer arc across the sky, New Hampshire begins to warm. Vegetation once buried under snow begins to show signs of coming out of its dormancy. Birds scout out sites for their nests. Spring is in the air.

Businesses make plans to accommodate tourists who will come to enjoy the scenic natural wonders and man-made attractions of New Hampshire. Thousands of miles of trails are inspected for repairs or clearing. Seacoast stores restock inventories in anticipation of the sun worshippers who will flock to New Hampshire's eighteen miles of clean coastline.

At Hampton Beach, world-class sand sculptors compete for monetary prizes and show what they can do with a ten-ton pile of sand. The results are unbelievable and remain displayed for about ten days, weather permitting.

Limited schedules for train rides typically begin in late April or May for the Cog Railway, Conway Scenic Railroad, Hobo Railroad, and Winnipesaukee Scenic Railroad. The M/S Mount Washington begins runs on Lake Winnipesaukee to Wolfeboro and Alton Bay from its home dock at Weirs Beach. Other attractions opening in May include the Mt. Washington Auto Road, Cannon Mountain Tramway, and Clark's Trading Post, with its trained bear show and White Mountain Railroad.

Sunrise at Island Pond, Stoddard

Albany Covered Bridge

State Capitol, Concord

Stone arch bridge, Hillsborough

Hikers take a well-deserved break on top of Mount Cardigan.

A foggy morning in Sugar Hill

New Hampshire has eighteen miles of coastline.

The M/S *Mount Washington* makes daily summer runs from Weirs Beach to ports in Wolfeboro and Alton Bay.

The only surviving iron smelter in New Hampshire is in Franconia.

Paradise Falls, Lost River Gorge

Nesting pairs of bald eagles are on the increase throughout New Hampshire.

Weeks State Park, Lancaster

Wentworth By The Sea Marina, New Castle

The heart and gathering place of each town—the village store

Portsmouth

Tamworth

Mount Chocorua as viewed from the Remick farm in Tamworth

Ashuelot Bridge features a covered walkway on both sides.

Keene

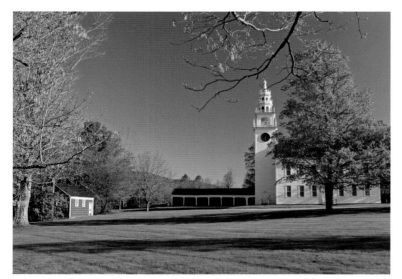

Jaffrey Center

Flume Brook flows through a gorge in Dixville Notch.

A hike up Wantastiquet Mountain leads to a lookout with a view of Brattleboro, Vermont.

World-class sand sculptors compete each year at Hampton Beach.

Mount Washington is the highest point in the Northeast; only hardy vegetation can survive on the summit.

Stoddard

Harrisville

Apple blossoms put on a show at a Hollis farm.

Sculptured Rocks Natural Area, Groton

One of two railroad covered bridges across the Sugar River between Newport and Claremont

Temple

Newport Town Common

Ashland

Hancock

The Mount Willard Trail ends at this scenic view of Crawford Notch.

Rowell's Covered Bridge, West Hopkinton

Blair Covered Bridge spans the Pemigewasset River near exit 27 of I-93.

A flowering tree hides a portion of the twenty-seven historical horse sheds behind Lyme Congregational Church.

Summer

Officially, summer begins around June 21. Unofficially, it begins Memorial Day weekend, as all attractions open seven days a week to accommodate those who come to experience New Hampshire.

Hikers are out in droves, whether their goal is one of our forty-eight 4,000-footers or just a relaxing walk in the woods. Weekend parking at the more popular trailheads, such as Mt. Major in Alton, Mt. Monadnock in Jaffrey, or West Rattlesnake in Holderness, can be problematic; a weekday trek may be a better option. Whether the trail is marked or unmarked, it is probably safe to say that there is an established route to the top of every mountain in the state.

The seacoast comes alive in the Hampton Beach area, as it becomes bustling and vibrant with visitors. Fireworks shows are staged Wednesdays and holidays. Tour boats cast out to Star Island from Portsmouth to see the grand hotel and other historic buildings. Tourists enjoy quaint New Castle village and Portsmouth Harbor Lighthouse.

Inland activities abound, with county fairs, festivals, and town parades typically happening on major holidays. Of special interest might be the wooden boat festival held at one of the marinas on Lake Winnipesaukee. Or consider a drive on the auto toll road to the top of Mount Washington, the highest point in the Northeast.

Balloons over the Suncook River at the annual Hot Air Balloon Rally in Pittsfield

Lake Solitude from Mount Sunapee

Waters of the Ammonoosuc River rush over the dam in Bath.

Barnstead awakes to a foggy morning.

Powder Mill Pond, Greenfield

Stratham Fair

Baling hay, Lyndeborough

Sawyers Crossing Covered Bridge, Swanzey

United Methodist Community Church, Monroe

A great blue heron rookery at the Monson Village historical site in Hollis

United Baptist Church, Lakeport

The Conway Scenic Railroad Notch Train passes through a narrow opening in the mountain near the train station in Crawford Notch State Park.

Portsmouth Harbor Lighthouse, New Castle

Sunrise at Hampton Beach

Lupine blooming along Route 302 in Bretton Woods

Hike to the top of any bald mountain and you may find the inscription of one who came before you.

Artist's Bluff provides a great view of Franconia Notch and the ski slopes on Cannon Mountain.

The Annual Lake Winnipesaukee Antique and Classic Boat Show

Fireworks over Hampton Beach are a summer tradition.

Newbury

Star Island, one of nine islands that make up the Isle of Shoals, is a bit over five miles offshore from Portsmouth.

The village of Orford and the Connecticut River seen from the Palisades in Fairlee, Vermont.

Riverwalk Covered Bridge provides pedestrians safe access to the heart of Littleton.

A stone wall, red barn, and beautiful view—quintessential New Hampshire

Wild roses populate seacoast shrubs.

The first Concord Stagecoach was built in 1827, by the Abbot Downing Company, and several examples are preserved within the state.

Summer parades such as this one in New Boston bring our rural communities together.

The Tall Ships Celebration in Portsmouth is a popular event.

The golden top of the capitol building

The restored home and windmill of Isaac Adams in Sandwich

This unusual stone wall is made from the foundation walls of neighboring residences in Sandwich purchased and razed by Isaac Adams.

Zip lines provide a summer activity for many of New Hampshire's ski slopes.

Loon

Acworth

Franconia Notch viewed from Cannon Mountain

Sunapee Harbor

Sunapee outlet footbridge over Sugar River

Tannery Hill Covered Footbridge in Gilford

Fall

For some it is a vacation they have intended to take for years, while others consider autumn in New Hampshire an annual pilgrimage. Crisp cool mornings, fresh apple cider donuts, annual craft fairs, and a seemingly endless orange, red, green, and yellow color palette covering the landscape make fall a truly wonderful time.

While trying to visit an area at its peak color is an elusive goal, there are some general observations that hold true. The Great North Woods (the part of New Hampshire north of the White Mountains) starts turning first, with much color showing at the end of September. Higher elevations in the White Mountains also have high color levels in late September, with lower levels following seven to ten days later. The Monadnock Region (southwest New Hampshire) is usually best around Columbus Day weekend. The seacoast and southeast portions of the state can retain color into early November. Several weather-related factors throughout the year can cause these generalities to be off target by one or two weeks.

Drive one of the Department of Tourism's suggested loops to experience idyllic villages in the Monadnock Region, take a route through the notches in the White Mountains, or plan a drive through Dixville Notch up to Pittsburg, then along Moose Alley (Route 3) to the Canadian border. A word of advice would be to book your lodging well in advance.

Center Sandwich

Fly fishing in the Great North Woods, Pittsburg

Restored Sandown Depot railroad station

Connecticut River cascade near First Connecticut Lake

Hebron

Pumpkin people appear in several towns during fall.

Lower Ammonoosuc Falls

The Balsams Resort and Lake Gloriette in Dixville Notch

Great North Woods as seen from Sanguinary Ridge in Dixville Notch

Berlin

Wood is stocked to the rafters for the next maple sap season.

Sumac shows its fall color.

Contoocook River, Francestown

Upper Ammonoosuc Falls, Crawford's Purchase

The view of Stark from the top of Devil's Slide

Stark

Jericho Lake, Berlin

An iron relic rests in a field along Route 26.

Mechanic Street Covered Bridge, Lancaster

The Cog Railway's steam engine begins its early morning ascent of Mt. Washington.

Saco River Covered Bridge, Conway

View of the Osceola Range from the Hancock Overlook along the Kancamagus Highway

Norway Pond, Hancock

Stonehouse Pond, Barrington

St. Matthews Chapel, Sugar Hill

View of Route 26 winding through Dixville Notch from Table Rock

Connecticut River near Pittsburg

Cathedral Ledge, North Conway

Crystal Falls, Stark Township

South Ponds, Stark

Lyndeborough Center

View from Square Ledge, Pinkham Notch

Packard Hill Covered Bridge, Lebanon

View from Abenaki Tower, Tuftonboro

Franconia Notch from Kinsman Trail on Cannon Mountain

Sunrise on Grafton Pond

Beaver Brook Falls, Colebrook

Tamworth

Cannon Mountain Gondola

Ken Paulsen was raised in the Midwest, where he worked most of his life in the information technology field prior to becoming a corporate instructor in South Carolina. He now resides in northern New England, where he has pursued his interest in photography, concentrating primarily on landscape scenes. His focus on the New England fall experience led to prior books *New Hampshire: An Autumn Sojourn*, *Vermont: An Autumn Perspective*, and *Vermont: A Focus on Fall*.

Welcome to
WINDHAM
Settled

Welcome to
Newport
Incorporated 1761

Welcome to
NEWMARKET
Founded in 1638
Incorporated 1727

WELCOME HISTORIC
PENACOOK VILLAGE

Welcome to
CAMPTON
Please Keep Our Community Clean!
Inc. 1767

GROVETON
COMMUNITY
WELCOMES YOU
TOWN OF
NORTHUMBERLAND
INCORPORATED
1761

Welcome To
WEARE, N.H.
INCORPORATED 1764
"A Part of Yesterday In Touch With Tomorrow."
Compliments of Weare Area Chamber of Commerce

Welcome to
•TAMWORTH•
Chartered 1766

WELCOME TO
SOMERSWORTH
NEW HAMPSHIRE
ESTABLISHED 1729

Welcome
to
Manchester
The Queen City

Welcome to
TOWN OF
STRATHAM
EST. 1716

Welcome
TO
NORTH
HAVERHILL
New Hampshire

WELCOME TO
LINCOLN
NEW HAMPSHIRE
In the White Mountains

WELCOME TO
PITTSBURG
NEW HAMPSHIRE
Established
1840

Welcome to
SHELBURNE

Welcome to the
Town of Stark

Welcome To
CORNISH
NEW HAMPSHIRE

WELCOME TO
HENNIKER

CONTENTS

First published 1979

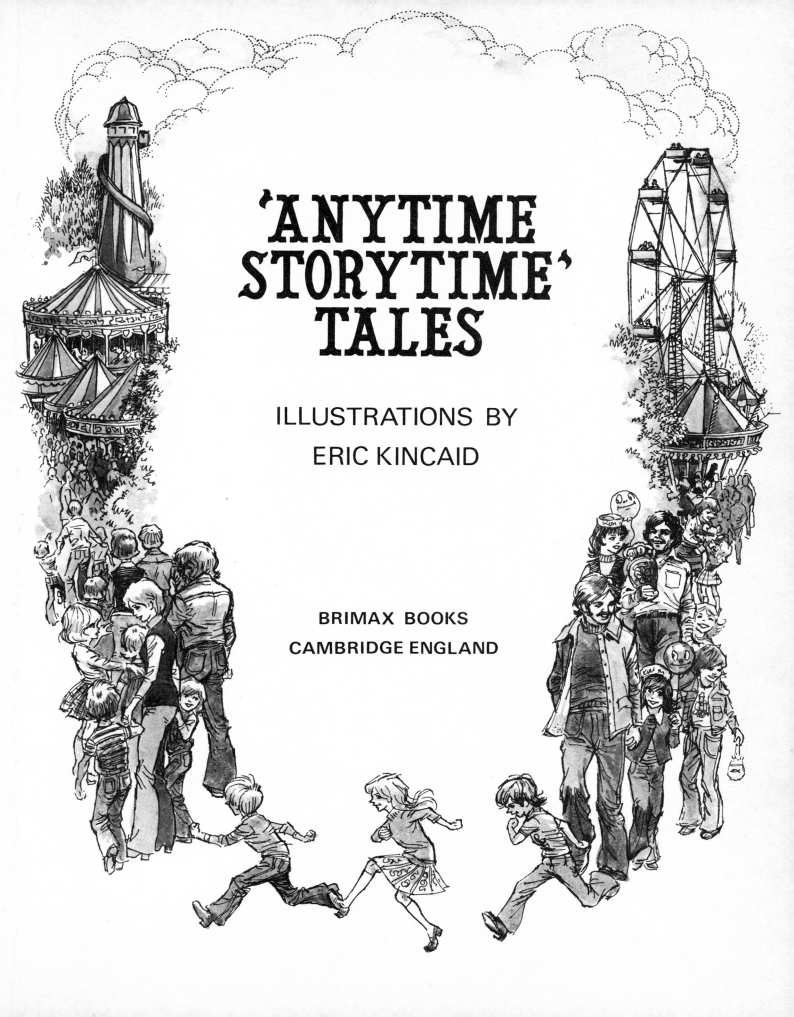

'ANYTIME STORYTIME' TALES

ILLUSTRATIONS BY

ERIC KINCAID

BRIMAX BOOKS

CAMBRIDGE ENGLAND

CHUFFA AND THE BANDIT

Way up in the North there is a great big fir forest, and in the forest there are many wild creatures like birds and bees, and butterflies and rabbits, and badgers and beavers and bears. There is also a railway line for carrying logs from the fir forest. And on this line goes Chuffa the train, driven by old Mr Driver. He is always ready to give anyone a lift and all the animals love him. And Chuffa too! Chuff chuff chuffa-chuffa-chuffa.

Now, one day some little birds flew up and said, "Oh, Mr Driver, do come and have a look at Bruin the Bear. He is very sick."

Mr Driver jammed on the brakes. ('I wish he wouldn't do that,' thought Chuffa.) Old Mr Driver got down from the train and the birds led him into the forest. There was Bruin the Bear propped up against a fir tree looking, very, very sick.

"Why, what's up Bruin?" asked Mr Driver.

But Bruin could only sigh. "Just hand me your paw," said old Mr Driver, and he took out his watch and felt Bruin's pulse.

"My, my, that's very fast, or else my watch is slow. You certainly are a sick bear. We shall have to get you to old Doc. Sawbones. He'll fix you up in a jiffy."

Well, it wasn't all that easy getting Bruin on the train. He was weak and limp and floppy and they had to pull him and push him and lift him.

"Gee, I feel sick," said Bruin.

"Never you mind, old fellow," said old Mr Driver. "Just a few more steps and you'll soon be on the train and on your way to the Doctor." At last they managed to shove him and push him and pull him into an empty truck.

"Ready?" said Mr Driver to Chuffa.

"Wooo-oo-oo," replied Chuffa and off they went. Chuffa-chuff-achuff-achuff-achuffa.

And of course they were late! The Station Master at Dallas was as cross as can be. "Just look at the time," he shouted. "Half an hour late! Half an hour!"

"I'm sorry. I couldn't help it," said Mr Driver. "I found a sick bear." And he showed the Station Master poor old Bruin. But that didn't please the Station Master either.

"Get that darned bear out of here," he yelled.

"I cannot," said Mr Driver. "He cannot walk and I cannot lift him. He is too sick to walk."

"Then put him on a trolley. Do anything but get him out of here. Do you hear?"

"Yes," said old Mr Driver.

Doctor Sawbones was very wise and he didn't mind seeing a great, big bear in his office. He looked at Bruin and listened to his chest and checked his tongue and felt his pulse and took his temperature. Then he said, "Hm," very wisely. "Hm, had any honey lately?"

The bear groaned. "Honey?" he said weakly. "Did you say honey? Well, perhaps just a taste."

"How much?" asked the Doctor.

"Well, w-e-l-l, about two pounds, maybe three," said the poor, sick bear.

"Right, into bed for three days. That'll put you right. And no more honey for a month."

And just as the Doctor said, in a few days the bear was quite well again and fit enough to go back to the forest. So old Mr Driver fetched Chuffa along and they set off for the fir forest. Chuff chuff chuffa chuffa-chuffa . . .

When they got there the bear climbed down and said to kind-hearted Mr Driver, "Thank you very much for helping me when I was sick. If ever you are in this forest and want any help, just call out 'Bruin' and I'll be there at once."

"Well, that is very kind of you," said Mr Driver. "I do hope I shall not need to call for help."

"So do I," said Bruin, "but you never can tell."

Back at the railway station, the Sheriff had a job for Mr Driver and Chuffa.

"Just listen to the Sheriff," said the Station Master. (But someone else was listening to the Sheriff. Who could it be?)

"I want you to take this bag of money to Woodville, see?" said
the Sheriff. (But someone else saw as well. Who could it be?)

"See no one steals it. Understand?" (But someone else understood
as well! Who could it be?) Mr Driver said he would take the money
for the Sheriff.

He took the money in the bag and hid it under some logs in the
train. Then he pulled the lever and off they went. C-h-u-f-f
chuff chuffa chuffa-chuffa . . .

All was going well as they went whisking through the forest, when
suddenly Chuffa saw a great pile of logs ahead right on the railway
line. He whistled like anything and Mr Driver jammed on the brakes.
('I wish he wouldn't do that,' thought Chuffa.)

Mr Driver got down and looked at the logs. "Something strange
going on down here," he said wisely. Then he began to shift the
logs from the line. Suddenly he heard a most terrible shout.

"STICK 'EM UP!" roared a voice.

And there beside the track was a bold, bad Bandit. With a bandit's horse. And a bandit's mask. And a bandit's gun! Poor Mr Driver had to put his hands up in the air.

"Now, where's that money?" shouted the Bandit.

"In the wood," said Mr Driver.

"And where's the wood?" cried the Bandit.

"Under the trees," said Mr Driver truthfully.

"Then I'll give you three seconds to find it," said that horrid Bandit, "Then, I'll fire."

So what could Mr Driver do but get the bag from under the wood.

"If you steal it, it won't do you any good you know," he said to the Bandit. "If you're a thief, you'll always find there's trouble brewing."

And as he said that, up popped Bruin the Bear! Like a flash he seized the bad Bandit's hat and pulled it down over his eyes.

At the sight of the bear, the bad Bandit's horse bolted, and the Bandit's gun went off BANG! But Bruin held on tight until Mr Driver brought a rope. Then they tied him up so that he could not escape and set him on top of some logs in one of the trucks.

"Come on Chuffa, my lad," said old Mr Driver. "Off we go to Woodville as quick as quick." Bruin said, "I think I'll get on as well, to keep an eye on this gentleman here." (He meant the Bandit.) So he got up on the next truck and kept a sharp eye on the Bandit who was too scared to move.

"Just as well you remembered to call out 'Bruin' like I said," said the bear.

"Wasn't it!" said Mr Driver who didn't know what he was talking about.

"Do you suppose there is a reward for this bandit?" Chuffa said. "Woo-oo-oo woo-oo-oo chuffa chuffa . . ."

When they reached Woodville, Mr Driver handed the money over to the Bank Manager. "Wonderful, wonderful," cried the Bank Manager. Then Mr Driver handed the Bandit over to the Sheriff. "Splendid, splendid," cried the Sheriff. Everyone in Woodville was delighted and there WAS a reward for the bold, bad Bandit. And the next day, Mr Driver and Bruin were given Sheriff's Deputy badges.

"I owe it all to Bruin," said Mr Driver.

"And I owe it all to Chuffa," said Bruin.

"And so do I," said Mr Driver, proudly patting Chuffa.

"Well done, Chuffa. Well done indeed."

THE THREE BILLY-GOATS GRUFF

Once upon a time and far, far, away, in a land of beautiful mountains, fine green fields and sparkling streams, there lived three billy-goats. They were all named Gruff.

The eldest and largest was called Big Billy-Goat Gruff; the next was called Middle Billy-Goat Gruff; and the youngest and smallest was called Tiny Billy-Goat Gruff.

They had eaten all the grass in their field; they were hungry and getting thinner every day. So, they set off to find a better place where they could eat and grow fat.

In the distance, on the other side of a wide stream, they saw a fine green field. The grass was thick and long; it looked absolutely delicious.

"We'd get fat on that," said Tiny Billy-Goat Gruff in his tiny voice.

"We certainly would," added Middle Billy-Goat Gruff in his middle-toned voice.

"We'll go!" declared Big Billy-Goat Gruff in his big gruff voice.

But, there was a bridge to be crossed and under that bridge there lived a troll. Now, trolls were the most objectionable creatures you could imagine. They were squat, with large ugly heads. They had great big staring eyes and enormous noses; their mouths were snarling and greedy; instead of finger nails and toe nails they had long sharp claws . . . Quite terrifying!

And the Troll under this bridge was the worst of all. No villagers or children ever tried to cross over. They were afraid of being gobbled up.

The three billy-goats looked at the bridge.

"How about the Troll?" asked Tiny Billy-Goat Gruff in his tiny voice.

"Yes, how about him?" added Middle Billy-Goat Gruff in his middle-toned voice.

"I have a plan," declared Big Billy-Goat Gruff in his big gruff voice. All three goats put their heads close together and they whispered to one another.

Tiny Billy-Goat Gruff was the first to reach the bridge. Trip, trip! went his tiny hooves on the wooden boards.

Out came the Troll.

"Who's that?" he roared. "Who's that tripping over my bridge?"

"Oh!" cried Tiny Billy-Goat Gruff in his tiny voice, "I'm Tiny, the smallest Billy-Goat Gruff. I'm going to the field to eat and grow fat."

"Ha!" roared the Troll again. "AND I'M GOING TO EAT YOU!"

Poor Tiny Goat trembled all over.

"Oh, no! Don't you bother with me . . . I'm very small and so thin! Why not wait for the next Billy-Goat Gruff; he's much bigger and fatter."

The Troll stopped to think.

"Very well!" he shouted. "Be off with you!"

So, Tiny Billy-Goat Gruff tripped over the bridge and into the fine green field.

Before long, up came Middle Billy-Goat Gruff. Trip, trot! Trip, trot! went his hooves on the wooden boards. Out came the Troll.

"Who's that?" he roared. "Who's that trotting over my bridge?"

"Oh!" cried Middle Billy-Goat Gruff in his middle-toned voice, "I'm Middle, the second Billy-Goat Gruff. I'm going to the field to eat and grow fat."

"Ha!" roared the Troll again. "AND I'M GOING TO EAT YOU!"

Poor Middle Goat trembled all over.

"Oh, no! Don't you bother with me . . . I'm only middle-sized and quite thin. Why not wait for Big Billy-Goat Gruff; he's really big and very much fatter."

The Troll stopped to think.

"Very well!" he shouted. "Be off with you!"

So, Middle Billy-Goat Gruff trotted over the bridge and into the fine green field.

Then came Big Billy-Goat Gruff. Trip, trot, tramp! Trip, trot, tramp! went his big hooves on the wooden boards. Out came the Troll.

"Who's that?" he roared louder than ever. "Who's that tramping over my bridge?"

"Ah!" answered Big Billy-Goat Gruff in his biggest, gruffest voice. "I'm Big, the biggest Billy-Goat Gruff . . . AND I'M TRAMPING OVER THIS BRIDGE!"

The Troll nearly roared his head off. "Then I'm coming to get you!" and he moved a few steps towards the goat.

"Oh, no you won't!" bellowed Big Billy-Goat Gruff. "I'M COMING TO GET YOU!"

He lowered his head and stamped his hooves. Tramp, tramp, TRAMP! Tramp, tramp, TRAMP!

They met and the battle began.

Big Billy prodded the Troll with his sharp horns, picked him up and tossed him into the air. The Troll turned three somersaults before he splashed down below into the deep water. He was never seen again.

So, Big Billy-Goat Gruff tramped across the bridge and into the fine green field.

All three billy-goats ate the sweet grass and grew fatter and fatter.

All the villagers and children were happy again. They could use the bridge, for the Troll was not there to gobble them up.

And all you children can sleep safe and sound, for there is not one single troll left — not anywhere.

THE WEDDING

One day, a little field mouse sat in the middle of a cornfield and waited for her friend Tom. He had a secret to tell, which he whispered in her ear, before they ran off together.

At the edge of the field, grew Red Poppy, now wide awake in the warm September sun. "Good morning," she said to the corn. "You do look well today, quite golden brown in fact."

"I know," said the corn. "And soon I shall be cut down and sent to the miller to be made into flour, but not before the wedding I hope."

"The wedding!" cried Red Poppy looking up at him.

"I use my ears, you know," he said. "Why, only last week I heard Tom Field Mouse telling Milly Field Mouse, that when the moon was full and round in the sky, they would be married the next day, at two o'clock."

"Why, that's today," said Red Poppy, dancing in the breeze.

The little blue flowers, standing on their thin stems said, "We shall ring for them this afternoon."

The little sparrows, sitting on top of the corn ears said, "We shall sing for them this afternoon."

"What can we do for them, Red Poppy?" asked the grass growing in the field.

"I'll ask the breeze to help you," she replied.

All week the little field mice had been collecting seeds and berries to eat at the Wedding Day party, and they had asked their cousins from town to come to the wedding and now, all was ready.

The village clock struck two – Tom and Milly Field Mouse were married. As they walked down the path by Red Poppy, the flowers began to ring, the sparrows began to sing and the breeze blew grass seed confetti all over them.

Then the party began. There was plenty to eat and then everyone played Hide and Seek, Hunt the Acorn and even had a climbing race to the top of the corn stalks.

"What a lovely wedding we have had," said Milly Field Mouse. "I wonder though, who told our secret."

"Oh, you can't have a secret here, my dear, remember the corn has ears," said Tom and quickly they ran away.

Now, the sun was going down and it was very quiet.

"Goodnight, Red Poppy," said the corn. "I wonder what I shall hear tomorrow?" Red Poppy did not answer, she was fast asleep.

DIFFY

Mrs Duck was very happy. She was listening to the little creaks and cracks that meant her eggs were breaking open and soon there would be a family of baby ducklings. One of the eggs kept rolling away and that one did not make any sound at all.

"Now WHY?" Mrs Duck asked herself, staring hard at it.

CREAK! CRACK! POP! went all the other eggs and out popped the fluffy yellow ducklings.

"BEAUTIFUL!" sighed Mrs Duck, happily. She glared at the egg that was left unopened as it rolled away uncracked.

SNAP! Without any warning at all the last egg BURST open and the duckling inside it SHOT out. He went up into the air as if he were a bird who could fly but not swim, instead of a bird that could swim but not fly. Mrs Duck watched open-beaked as the youngest duckling soared into space.

"NOT a budding space-duck!" wailed Mrs Duck, who sometimes watched the Farmer's television.

But the little fellow soon came down to earth again because, of course, he could NOT fly, and he landed upside-down next to his brothers and sisters.

Mrs Duck eyed her son fondly.

"I thought YOU would be different," she said, not knowing whether to be proud or put-out.

"DIFFERENT!" gurgled the little duckling. "What a lovely name. Call me DIFFY!"

The very first thing Diffy wanted to do was to leave home.

"You can't!" snapped Mrs Duck. "You've only just got here."

"I have a SPIRIT OF ADVENTURE," explained Diffy. He had a very good turn of speech, or rather, QUACK, for such a young duckling.

"Save it until you are grown up," shrieked Mrs Duck. She had to shriek because little Diffy was already on his way.

The first place brave Diffy came to was not as adventurous as he thought it might be. HE thought that after all that walking he must have reached foreign parts but he hadn't. He had only got as far as the farmhouse.

The farmer's wife was cleaning the kitchen. She did not like the job and so she was doing it as quickly as she could to get it over. She was rather short-sighted and so when Diffy perched on the handle of a wooden spoon for a rest, she thought he was a feather-duster.

"I had forgotten I had this," she told herself, as she picked up the DIFFYDUCKYWOODENSPOONFEATHERDUSTER.

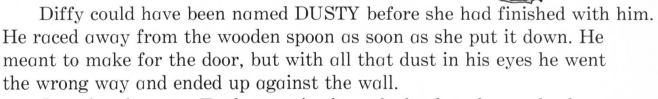

Diffy had to cling hard to that wooden spoon because first the farmer's wife shot him UP to dust the pictures. Then she pushed him SIDEWAYS to dust the clock and even DOWN to dust inside a vase.

Diffy could have been named DUSTY before she had finished with him. He raced away from the wooden spoon as soon as she put it down. He meant to make for the door, but with all that dust in his eyes he went the wrong way and ended up against the wall.

Just then her son, Fred, came in through the door from school. Fred did not see Diffy sitting on the floor trying to brush the dust out of his eyes. Fred took off his hat as soon as he came in, as he always did. He tossed it across the room to try and get it on the hook in the wall above where Diffy was, as he always did. Fred missed, as he always did. The hat fell on the floor as it always did. But never before had there been a baby duckling sitting there, as there was this time. The hat fell over Diffy and at once it did something it had NEVER done before. THE HAT RAN ACROSS THE FLOOR!

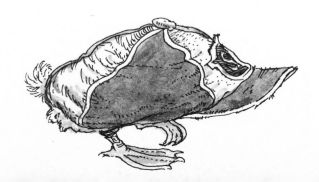

It was only Diffy really, who thought the roof had fallen on top of him and was running to try and shake it off. Fred thought that he was seeing MAGIC and he just stood and watched with eyes like saucers. He closed his eyes so that he could yell louder and at that very moment Diffy reached -- and fell over -- the doorstep. The hat stayed behind and Diffy was able to scuttle away. When Fred opened his eyes again after his yell, Diffy was gone.

For ever after, Fred was sure that he was the only person in the world who had seen a hat run across a floor. As a matter of fact, he wrote an essay about it at school the next day and got top marks for imagination.

Diffy left his SPIRIT OF ADVENTURE behind him in the farmhouse. He knew that his beak was pointed towards his duckpond home, because he could hear his mother telling his brothers and sisters what to do as she took them for their first swim.

Diffy decided to join them and go back later for his lost SPIRIT OF ADVENTURE. It was sad, in a way, because Mrs Duck could not count and she didn't have time to notice that Diffy was back again. She went on boasting dreadfully to friends and relations about her youngest son, who, she told them, was TRAVELLING THE WORLD WITH A SPIRIT OF ADVENTURE. None of the family and friends could count and so THEY did not know either that Diffy was back, which was a pity for them, because they did get so horribly bored just HEARING about him.

As for Diffy HE never tired of hearing about himself and as he listened hard ALL the time, he grew up feeling that he really was DIFFERENT!

THE MOUSE

A little mouse hid himself under a chair,
He knew, of course, who was sitting there;
A gracious lady – so calm and serene,
Robed and bejeweled – a beautiful Queen.

He wanted to see all the people who came;
All were important – some of great fame;
The colors and costumes! A splendid sight!
But then the mouse had a terrible fright.

For someone had joined him, the Right Royal Cat:
"What do you think you are playing at?
A mouse –– in the palace! It will not do!
My duty is plain –– I'm kept to kill you."

The brave little mouse tried to smile a faint smile:
"Your Highness, could you not wait awhile?
I'm really quite thin -- a very poor snack;
I'm afraid I shall scream when you attack."

"Very well," said the cat, "we'll see out the ball;
Can't let a mouse cause chaos, at all:
But when it's done and the Queen goes to bed;
I tell you, mouse, you'll be deader than dead!"

The cat settled down and the mouse looked around;
A way to escape, it must be found!
The hem of Her Majesty's gown of lace,
He chewed the stitches and squeezed in the space.

So when the dear Queen thought she'd had quite enough,
Mouse went too – leaving cat in a huff.
"A fine stately ride! Three squeaks for that!
The Queen! God Bless Her! We fooled the cat!"

THE NEW COAT

Pimm Pixie was rolling up cobweb thread in the brambles one day, when his coat caught on a thorn, and tore from the collar right down to the hem. It was as open down the back as it was down the front.

"I suppose I could put some buttons on it," he said, "but then everyone would think I had my head on back to front."

When he got home he mended the tear but he knew the coat would never be the same.

"I can't see the mend myself," he said, "but everyone else can. Everyone will be looking at my stitches, which I know are very uneven. I think it's time I had a new coat."

He went to see the pixie tailor.

"Good morning Pimm," said the tailor. "What can I do for you?"

"I want a new coat, exactly like this one," said Pimm. The torn coat had a deep collar to turn up round his ears when the wind blew, it was long enough to keep his knees warm, and it had deep pockets for carrying things in. He felt comfortable in it. He liked wearing it and saw no reason why his new coat should be any different.

"I'll be glad to make it for you," said the tailor, who had made Pimm's first coat and was glad he liked it so much. He took Pimm's measurements, just to make sure they were still the same, which they were, pixies not being in the habit of growing very much.

"There is one small change I would like you to make," said Pimm, who had been looking at the tailor's own coat.

"Yes?" said the tailor, waiting with his pencil held over his note pad.

"I would like it made up in a different shade of green this time . . . I like the shade you are wearing."

The tailor wrote, 'color, emerald green' on his note pad.

"When will it be ready?" asked Pimm. His own sewing was not very good. The draughts were finding their way in, in between his clumsy stitches and his back was getting cold.

"Tomorrow, if I start straight away," said the tailor, and he went to the shelf and took down a roll of emerald green cloth.

"Ummmm" said Pimm thoughtfully, as the tailor started to snip with his scissors. Pixie tailors can start cutting straight away, they don't have to bother with paper patterns. "Perhaps that blue would be better."

"But I've already started cutting," said the tailor.

"It's my coat. I'm the one who will have to wear it. The color MUST be right.

The tailor put down his scissors. "If you want your coat finished by tomorrow," he said, "you must make up your mind quickly. I will give you until eleven o'clock."

"I'll go away, and think about it, and then come back and tell you what I have decided," said Pimm. Before he reached the door he turned and said, "I've thought already. Make it in crimson."

"Very well . . . if you're QUITE sure," said the tailor.

Pimm said he WAS sure, but five minutes later he was back. "I've changed my mind. I'll have it made in yellow."

Ten minutes later he had decided on indigo. And ten minutes after that, he had decided on purple.

"I do wish you'd make up your mind," sighed the tailor.

"I am making up my mind," said Pimm. "I've made it up six times already."

The tailor put ALL the rolls of cloth on the table.

"Now which is it to be?" he said, beginning to look almost as sharp and scratchy as his pins. "I can't have you changing your mind any more. I have other customers to think about."

"The trouble is," wailed Pimm, "I like ALL the colors. It really is very difficult to choose just one."

"Then leave the choice to me," said the tailor. It seemed to Pimm that perhaps that might be the best idea.

"Come back in the morning," said the tailor. "If I see your nose peeping round that door before morning I'll snip it off with my scissors." He didn't mean that of course, but he had to keep Pimm out of his way somehow. "Now be off with you!"

Pimm hardly slept a wink all night wondering what color cloth the tailor would use.

Next morning, as soon as it was light, he went and stood on the tailor's doorstep. It was hours before the tailor opened the door. He knew Pimm was there, but he had his breakfast first, swept the floor and tidied the shelves. He didn't think it would do Pimm any harm to keep him waiting. At nine o'clock precisely, by the dandelion clock, he unbolted the door and let Pimm in.

"Is it finished? What color did you use? Let me see it. Oh, I do hope you used the RIGHT color!"

"Which color IS the right color?" asked the tailor.

"I don't know . . . if only I DID know . . ." wailed Pimm.

He could hardly bear to look as the tailor uncovered the coat. What could he say if he didn't like the color the tailor had chosen? But what a surprise he had. He gasped! He clasped his hands together in glee! He jumped onto the table and danced a jig! He beamed from ear to ear! The point on his hat curled and uncurled by itself! The tailor looked pleased.

"Did I use the right color?" he asked, dodging out of the way as Pimm bounced up and down like a ball.

"Oh you did! You did!" exclaimed Pimm. "What a clever tailor you are!"

The tailor blushed with pleasure.

"Try it on for size," he said. It fitted perfectly, as he knew it would because he had taken the measurements himself.

"Thank you . . . thank you . . . thank you . . ." sang Pimm as he danced off down the street. The clever tailor had used a piece of cloth from each roll and had made him a coat that was ALL colors of the rainbow!

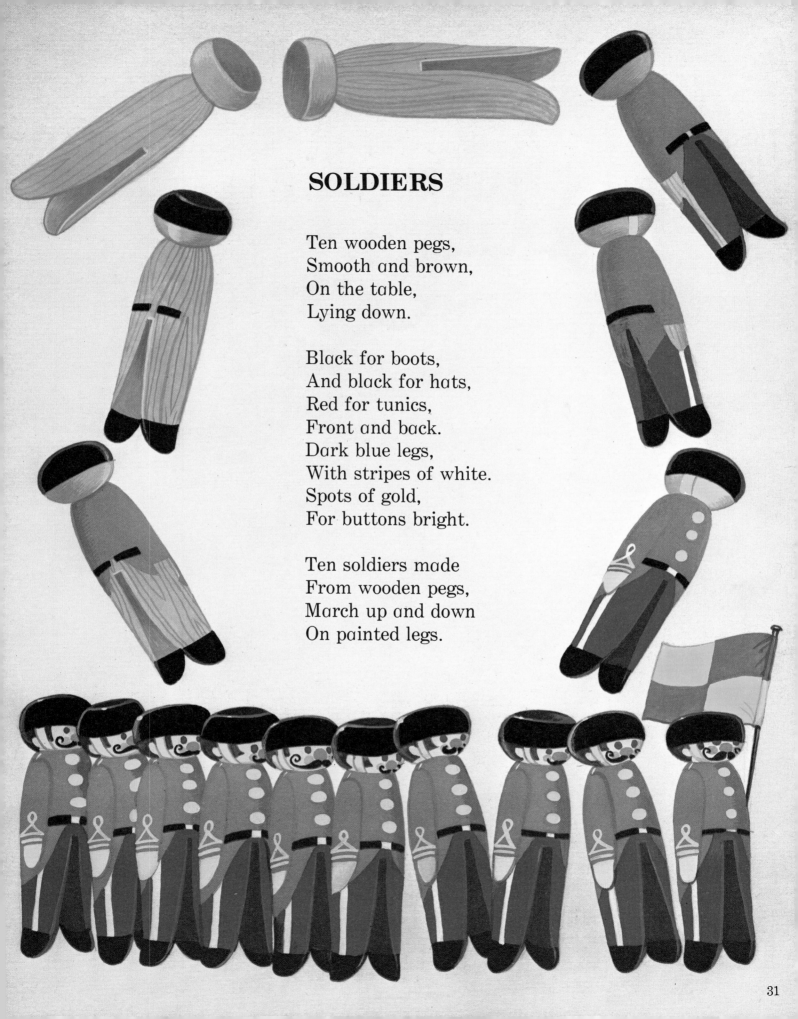

SOLDIERS

Ten wooden pegs,
Smooth and brown,
On the table,
Lying down.

Black for boots,
And black for hats,
Red for tunics,
Front and back.
Dark blue legs,
With stripes of white.
Spots of gold,
For buttons bright.

Ten soldiers made
From wooden pegs,
March up and down
On painted legs.

FLY AWAY TERRY

Terry Towel was tired of being washed, and hung on the line to dry, every Monday morning. Soap made him sneeze, hot water made him limp, the spin dryer made him dizzy and the pegs pinched him. One Monday morning, when he had sneezed more than usual, and the pegs were pinching extra hard, he decided he could bear it no longer. He began to pull at the horrid pegs which were holding him so tightly to the line.

"Help me . . . help me . . ." he called to the wind. He pulled and he tugged and he wriggled. The wind was doing his best to help. He could feel one of the pegs loosening.

Ping! The loose peg flew off the line and lay in the grass.

'Nearly free . . . one more hard tug should do it,' thought Terry. He waited until the wind puffed out another gust, and then he pulled with all his might . . . and away he sailed, up, up, up, into the sky.

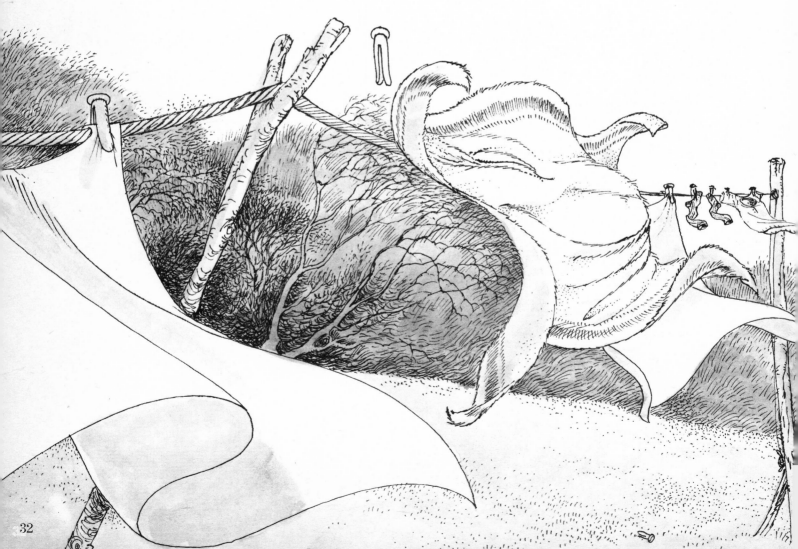

"I'm free . . . I'm free!" he called at the top of his voice.

Two birds flying by were taken completely by surprise.

"What do you suppose THAT was?" one of them chirped, turning his head to get a better look and bumping into his friend as he did so.

"Look where you're going . . ." twittered his friend with feathers all ruffled. "It's only a piece of blown-away-washing."

Terry didn't like being called a piece of blown-away-washing.

"Oh no I'm not . . . I'm King of the Sky!" he shouted.

"You're not!" twittered the birds.

"I am . . ." shouted Terry. "I am . . . I am . . . I am . . ." And he twisted and turned in loops and circles, and he dived and soared like a kite to show them how clever he was. "Look at me! Look at me!"

"Do stop showing off . . ." twittered the birds, who knew they could do everything Terry was doing, only better.

"I'm not showing off! I'm King of the Sky. You must all bow when I pass."

The birds ignored him, as he deserved, and flew away.

"It's only because you're jealous of me!" shouted Terry.

The wind, who had been listening, suddenly stopped blowing. The birds carried on flying of course, because they had their wings to carry THEM, but Terry went limp and fell to the ground.

"How dare you let me fall . . ." shouted Terry. "I'm King of the Sky. Blow wind . . . blow!"

"Only if you stop boasting," said the wind.

"I will . . . I will," said Terry. So the good-natured wind, puffed up his cheeks and blew Terry back into the air. Away danced Terry, skipping and hopping and looping over the grass.

"Moo . . ." hiccupped a cow, as Terry danced in front of her and dazzled her. "What's that?"

"A piece of blown-away-washing!" twittered the birds.

"Maa . . . ammma . . . wait for me . . . maa . . . baaaa . . ." bleated a tiny lamb, mistaking Terry for her mother, and running after him.

"Baaa . . . come back at once . . ." bleated the lamb's mother. "Can't you tell the difference between your own mother and a piece of blown-away-washing?"

Terry laughed. He was having fun.

He danced right across the
field and into the shady wood. He
danced in and out of the trees,
startling the rabbits, and
frightening the squirrels.
Presently he heard voices. There
were children walking amongst the
bluebells. One of the children
saw him, and screamed.

"It's a ghost!"
"Look! Look!"
"It's a ghost!"

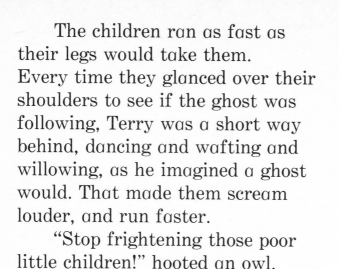

The children ran as fast as
their legs would take them.
Every time they glanced over their
shoulders to see if the ghost was
following, Terry was a short way
behind, dancing and wafting and
willowing, as he imagined a ghost
would. That made them scream
louder, and run faster.

"Stop frightening those poor
little children!" hooted an owl.

"I'm not frightening anyone," said Terry. "I didn't tell
them I was a ghost. I can't help it if they happen to think I
am." He followed the children all the way home. At their
garden gate, Rover, their dog came running to protect them. He
barked at Terry.

"Stop frightening my children . . . " he growled. He caught
hold of one of Terry's corners with his teeth and shook him.

"Put me down . . . put me down . . . " gasped Terry.

"Only if you behave yourself," said Rover, without letting
go.

"Look," said the children. "It wasn't a ghost at all. It's a piece of blown-away-washing. Let it go, Rover, there's a good boy. We're not afraid anymore."

Rover let go at once, and Terry fell to the ground with a sigh. Being shaken THAT hard didn't agree with him at all. The children came and picked him up. His back and his front were covered with dirty streaks where he had been playing in the field, and green streaks where he had rubbed against mossy bark in the wood. He looked a sorry sight. He felt a sorry sight.

The childrens' mother came into the garden.

"You've found my towel," she said. "It blew off the line this morning. I wondered where it had got to."

Once more, Terry found himself sneezing in the washing machine and getting dizzy in the spin dryer. But this time, as he hung on the line with the pegs pinching his corners, he decided that being soft, and clean, and fluffy, wasn't so bad after all, and when the wind asked him if he wanted to go for another fly around the sky, he said,

"No thank you. I've had my adventure, and I enjoyed it. I'm quite content to be myself now."

He danced on the line until he was dry, making quite sure he didn't pull at the pegs TOO hard. And then he was folded and put away in a warm cupboard -- a cleaner, and wiser towel.

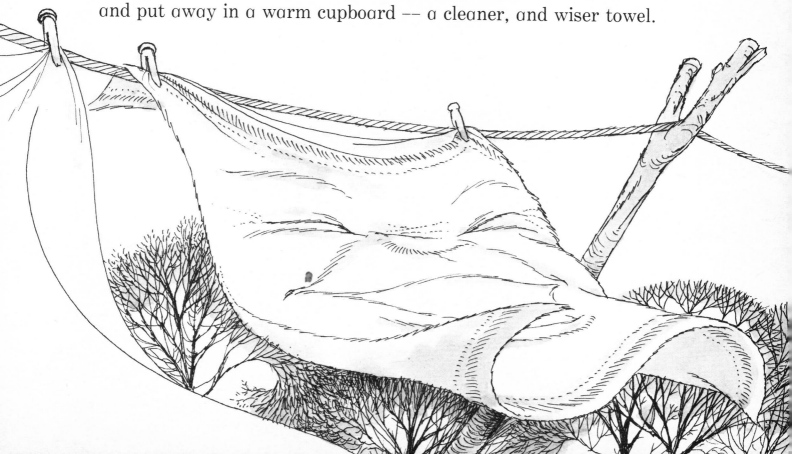

SPROGGET ON HOLIDAY

One day I called my special friend, Sprogget, the magic one;
Nobody knows about him, but he is lots of fun.
"Come, Sprog, the car is waiting! Please hurry or you'll find
That we have gone on holiday -- and you are left behind."

But Sprogget came and we set off through towns and country fine.
We climbed the hills; we followed streams; passed forests of dark pine.
At last we stopped at Granny's -- she opened up the gate.
"You'll love the farm," I whispered. "Oh, Sprog, it's really great!"

We had a meal -- a proper feast -- like in a fairy book;
Gran remembers things I like -- she knows just what to cook.
Then, out to see the animals -- a calf and a new foal;
I helped to feed the chickens and I filled their drinking bowl.

We slept that night in my small room -- kept specially for me;
I woke to hear the farm sounds -- saw Sprogget up a tree;
He'd swung himself out on a branch that tapped my window pane;
Throughout our stay, he used that way -- many times again.

We rode the Shetland pony and the donkey called Grey-Moke;
When I fell off, my Sprogget laughed -- he thought it was a joke.
I warned him, "Just you watch it! You might fall yourself one day!"
He winked at me and helped me up; then off we ran to play.

The day we went to market I thought my friend was lost;
He didn't join me shopping -- didn't help me check the cost.
Then suddenly he came along astride a baby goat;
He'd saved it from the river with a rope slipped round its throat.

Of course, no one could see or hear my magic Sprogget man;
Folk asked a lot of questions and marched me off to Gran;
The little kid was never claimed; Gran kept it on the farm
It's pretty -- we all love it and it's safe from any harm.

Our holiday is over , Why can't it last and last?
I've never known so many days go whizzing by so fast.
Granny's asked us back quite soon, to have a longer stay;
Sprogget grins and we both shout: "Hip, hip! Hip, hip! Hurray!"

TOM THE GIANT

Once upon a time, there was a giant. His name was Tom, and he lived all by himself in the mountains. His cabin was made of tall trees, his cup was as big as a barrel and his boots were as large as boats.

Tom was a very friendly giant, but the people who lived in the town nearby were afraid of him because he looked so big and fierce.

One day, Tom went into the town to buy some green wool to make himself a hat. As soon as the people saw him coming, they shut the gates of the town and ran into their houses to hide. Tom stepped over the wall, but when he walked along the street all the people shouted at him from their windows.

"Go away," they cried. "You are much too big to come into our town. You will tread on us and squash us flat."

At last, poor Tom had to go away without the wool for his hat, because none of the shopkeepers would sell him any. When he got home he took off his boots and lay down to sleep in his giant bed. Before long he was fast asleep, with his giant cat Toby curled up on the blanket beside him.

During the night, a terrible storm arose. The thunder rolled, the lightning flashed and the rain poured down like a waterfall. Then a terrible wind came which blew away all the black rain clouds and when there were no clouds left, it blew away the stars.

The stars fell down a hundred at a time. They sparkled through the air and landed as quietly as snow. They lay twinkling where they had fallen -- on the grass, in the fields, on the trees, in the streets and on all the rooftops in the town.

All the people were amazed when they saw the stars. They looked up into the dark and empty sky.

"How shall we put the stars back?" they said.

The next morning, the town crier went round the town ringing his bell. "Oyez, Oyez, Oyez," he cried. "If anyone can put the stars back into the sky he shall have a hundred pieces of gold as his reward."

Everyone tried to think of a way to put the stars back, but nobody had the faintest idea of what to do. No one thought of asking Tom the Giant.

"What on earth shall we do?" said the Lord Mayor.

"I don't know, I'm sure," said the town crier.

Just then, they heard the heavy footsteps of Tom the Giant.

"Don't be afraid," called Tom. "I have come to put the stars back, if you will help me."

One by one the people came out of their houses and stood on the walls to talk to Tom.

"What do you want us to do?" asked the Lord Mayor.

"Everyone must take a bag and pick up all the stars he can find," said Tom. "When all the stars have been picked up, bring them to me and I will take them away in my big leather sack ready to put them back in the sky."

No sooner said than done.
The people searched everywhere for
the fallen stars. They looked
under the bushes and in the flower
beds; they looked down the chimneys
and at the bottom of the wells,
until at last they had found every
single star. Then Tom emptied all
the bags of stars into his big sack.
He picked it up, and set out for the
mountains. All the people stood
on the walls and waved as he walked
away.

As soon as he reached his
cabin, Tom took down his long
ladder. Then he stood the ladder
against the clouds and climbed up
with the sack of stars on his
back. One by one he put all the
stars back into the sky. When
night came the stars twinkled as
merrily as ever, just as if nothing
had ever happened.

The next day, Tom went down to the town to see the people. They gave a loud cheer when they saw him.

"Here are your hundred pieces of gold," said the Lord Mayor.

"I do not want the gold," said Tom. "All I want is some green wool to make a hat."

The people took the wool from fifty sheep until they had enough to make a hat for Tom. They worked all day, and by that evening, a new green hat was ready for him.

"Thank you," said Tom. With the green hat on his head, he walked proudly back to his home in the mountains. The people were never afraid of him again.

AMANDA AND THE ANIMALS

Once upon a time, there was a little girl called Amanda, who lived in a pretty white house in the country with her mother and father.

One sunny day, as it was her birthday, and so, of course, a very special day, they took her to the zoo. Amanda was so excited, for it was the first time she had ever been there and she adored animals.

She gazed in wonder at the huge lions, laughed at the antics of the cheeky monkeys, and stroked the heads of the gentle deer. She had a wonderful time!

Later that day, tired but happy, she sat on her garden swing while her mother prepared supper –– a special birthday supper –– with a birthday cake as well.

Amanda swung slowly backwards and forwards, her mind full of all the animals she'd seen at the zoo, some so big; some so small; and all the time she swung, backwards and forwards, backwards and forwards . . .

'In the jungle, I'm a king,'
Remarked the Lion full of pride,
'I'm not afraid of anything,
At least, not much,' he said aside.

'I know the big savannah well,
There, many animals retreat.
But I must find out where they dwell,
For when I'm hungry, I must eat.'

Amanda's blue eyes widened as she looked at the lion. He
certainly was beautiful, with his thick golden mane and his
flashing eyes. As a matter of fact, he was sitting on her
father's prize roses, but she didn't like to tell him, in case
he was offended. He went on . . .

'My claws are very sharp, you know,
Because they have to grasp and tear.
My sense of smell is not so good,
But there's very little I don't hear.

At night, I see as well as day,
And I can run quite fast along,
Though rarely do I chase my prey,
For I am very, very strong.'

Another voice broke in then, and Amanda saw a giraffe looking
down at the lion, who was now busily washing his paws!

'What of me?' asked the Giraffe,
I'm very tall, quite eighteen feet.
My neck is long,' he gave a laugh,
'So from the tall trees I can eat.

My eyes are fringed against the sun.
I've two horns on my head.
I have no voice at all -- just none,
I cannot even howl instead!

I live in Africa -- it's hot,
The sun is always big and bright,
It seems to shine an awful lot,
The only time it's cool is night.

It's quite a problem when I drink,
I have to put my legs astride,
Yet though I'm tall, I really think
I'm quite content and satisfied.'

Amanda chuckled at this, then stared in surprise at the zebra who was standing there listening with much attention.

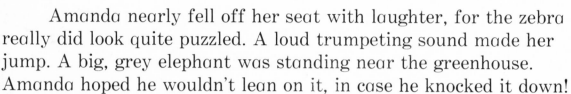

'My stripes blend in with the trees,
And with the background where I live.
I come and go just as I please,
Though lots of care to this I give!'

On one point I should like some light
About these stripes upon my back.
Now what is which, I don't know quite—
Black stripe on white or white on black?'

Amanda nearly fell off her seat with laughter, for the zebra really did look quite puzzled. A loud trumpeting sound made her jump. A big, grey elephant was standing near the greenhouse. Amanda hoped he wouldn't lean on it, in case he knocked it down!

'In size I'm larger than you all,
For quite six tons -- that's what I weigh.
I trumpet loudly when I call,
So they can hear me far away.

You'd think my trunk was in the way,
And yet without it lost I'd be,
For when I'm hungry through the day,
I pick leaves from the highest tree.

Some of my friends, they work for man,
They pull and lift the trunks of trees,
That's not for me, for if I can
I'd rather do just what I please.'

The elephant thought hard for a moment, swinging his trunk from side to side, until Amanda knew she'd simply burst if she didn't laugh soon, but she didn't dare!

The elephant continued,

'My ears are big; my hide is grey,
I have two tusks of ivory;
I've nothing really more to say,
Except I'm rather glad I'm me!'

Here he was interrupted by a sniffly, snuffly sort of voice.

'I know I am an ugly beast,
But all Hippos are just like me;
And I don't mind it in the least,
There's nothing else I'd rather be!

You'd see that just my head appears
When I am swimming, which I love;
For I also close my nose and ears,
That's all you notice from above.'

The hippopotamus stopped short then, his words almost drowned when he opened his enormous mouth to have a big, comfortable yawn! Amanda couldn't believe her eyes. How could any animal have such a huge mouth?

'I'm twelve feet long, that's quite a lot,
I weigh four tons, or so it's said.
My feet are webbed, so I can trot
Along the muddy river-bed.

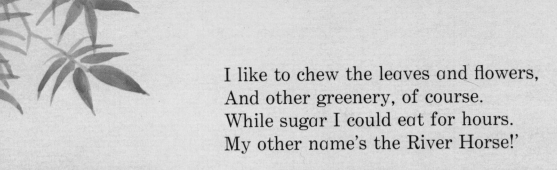

I like to chew the leaves and flowers,
And other greenery, of course.
While sugar I could eat for hours.
My other name's the River Horse!'

Amanda was surprised to hear this, and thought it was a lovely name. The Hippo looked at her, his little eyes twinkling, gave another yawn, and promptly went to sleep!

There was a sudden thud, and a kangaroo appeared from nowhere!

'I know I'm not as big as you,
Nor quite as heavy, nor as plump;
But there's one thing that you can't do,
That I can do, and that is JUMP!

I leap as far as twenty feet,
The farmers wish I could be banned,
Because you see, I love to eat
The grass that grows upon their land.

When I was born, you'd never dream
That I was very, very small,
So very tiny, it would seem
I wasn't really there at all!

Within my mother's pouch I kept,
Though that's a long time past, I own.
Inside it, nice and warm I slept,
But now I'm big and fully-grown.'

Even as he finished, all the other animals who had been listening, started to make such a noise, each one claiming that he was the finest animal. Amanda put her hands on her ears to shut out the noise, but it grew louder and louder, until suddenly she heard above it all, someone calling her name.

"Amanda, supper's ready!" It was her mother calling. She turned to look at the animals again, but they all seemed to have disappeared somewhere.

"What a shame," she said, "I was so enjoying myself!" She raced down the garden path and went into the house.

"Mommy, I've just seen some of the animals that we saw at the zoo today!" Amanda told her excitedly.

Her mother smiled down at her. "Oh, Amanda," she laughed, "have you been playing make-believe again?" Amanda opened her mouth to argue, but shut it again. She knew it wasn't any good anyway, because whenever she'd had an adventure before, and told her mother, she'd always said Amanda had been playing make-believe. Grown-ups didn't know everything, did they?